The Living Breath
100 Psalms

Jesus Christ,
my Great God and Savior

Yongjea John Han

Copyright © 2018 Yongjea John Han

First edition

Designed and Edited by Canada Christian Society

All rights reserved. No part of this book may be reproduced or transmitted in any form or by any means, electronic or mechanical, including photocopying, recording, or by any information storage or retrieval system, without the prior written permission of CCS.

ISBN-13: 978-1-7750387-4-0

CONTENTS

Prologue   6

PART 1

Blessed Union   8
The Lord of Light   9
The Greatest   10
Faithfulness   11
Garden of Memory   13
In the Field   14
The Prayer of March   16
Praise of the Victory   18
Prayer in the Spring   20
Be Humble   21
The Life of the Evangelist   22
Prayer for the Oppressed   24
Prayer for Everyday life   26
A Prayer for Prosperity   28
Recovery from Mental Illness   29
Prayer for Child Raising   30
Palm Sunday Prayer   31
Crucified Week   32
In the Resurrection Power   33
On Easter Morning   34
Waiting for the Lord to come again   35
Pray for Husbands and Wives   37
Let me be a good parent.   38
Let me be the head of home.   39
Pray for the world   40
Prayer for the magistrates   41
Let me be a good teacher and a disciple   42
Heavenly Father of Power   44
Let us have a tolerance for others.   45

PART 2

Lord, where are you? 47
A true friend 48
The peace of John 14:27 49
The Lord always listens 50
Walk with the Lord 52
The heart of the Father who is perfect 53
This way 54
The Breath of Life 55
Living water 56
When life is desperate 58
A Suffering Conscience 59
Look at the Lord at the time of the test. 60
New Mission (Luke 24) 61
Almighty God 62
The Lord is my shelter. 63
In a dead end 64
Depend on 65
Leave my burden to the Lord. 67
A child of hope 68
Sail 69
Satisfaction towards the Lord 70
Cleansed Lips 71
The wickedness of the world is a moment. 72

PART 3

A Believing Family 74
God's Will 75
Rely on the Lord 76
Morning Meditation 77
A Warm Word 78

He keeps faith children. 79
The Lord who does not discriminate 80
A True Friend 81
Keep your heart. 82
The Lord came to this world 83
The Way of Life 84
Witness 85
Equability 86
I will let down the nets. 87
You know the wishes of the heart. 88
Praise be to the Lord for eternity 89
Way 90
New Creature 91
The Lord's Family 92

PART 4

Intercession 94
I will boast of You. 95
I want to hear the voice of the Lord. 96
Do not look back 97
O my soul, give thanks to the Lord. 98
Thanksgiving 99
My Children 100
Memory 101
A Wilderness Road 102
A Path 103
To Please Jehovah 104
The center of my heart 105
Birth of Jesus 106
Birth of a New Covenant 107
United to make good 108
Our Victory 109
Towards the Lord 111

The Lord comes again 112
Prayer 113
The Second Coming of the Lord 114
A word like dew 115
God of the Covenant 116
Hymn and Glory 117
Light of the World 118

Prologue

YOU ARE MY GREAT GOD AND MY SAVIOR. YOUR NAME CAN GIVE TO ME A TRUE WAY AND A LIFE. YOU ARE THE LIFE OF BREATH. YOUR NAME IS JESUS CHRIST. I WANT TO PRAISE WITH PSLAMS AND MY SOUL AND HEART.

PART 1

Blessed Union

Lord! when I think of the word love,
I feel so peaceful and joyful.
Love makes people free.
We know you're the love taking part in the free.
Neither of us are any good at planning,
but we believe in your good plan for us.
We want to dress with your love.
Some people see your noble sacrifice too lightly.
It is as if they think too lightly
about the marriage ceremony in love.
Too many people are breaking up
and breaking promises of blessed unity.
Lord! I hear rumors from the ungodly
from the world.
Just as the day of the Lord is fixed,
let us know that you have a blessed day of love.
I want to go to your love space.
We are your bride.
Jesus Christ!
Protect us from the world
to live a sanctified life.
We are holy people who made a reservation
for you with a marriage.
May you lead me to a blessed union
on a beautiful and sunny day.

The Lord of Light

Lord of love,
today I stand before your holiness.
The brilliant morning sun is
not as bright as yours.
Do not erase me in your memory.
Do not abandon me in the many times
I have lived until now,
always living in your light,
in a world without light,
like a child who was humble in the face of you,
take your word like the dew of the morning,
enjoying eternal life,
please let me live today.
Lord of love,
in the midst of the world,
you choose me,
you have made your word known.
Do not forget the moment you choose,
to those who do not know the light of the Lord,
let them know that life is not the end of the world.
I still remember you who lived poorly.
Your light has made us rich.
Thank you for your victory over the darkness.
Lord of love,
in a world full of darkness,
let me win by the light of the Lord.
Amen,

The Greatest

**Father, your wonderful grace
will become more plentiful.
Even we were born a sinner,
we believe in your doing for us,
grace, forgiveness and restoration.
Although we are being treated
as 'throw-away' in the earth,
and we are rooted in the desert
without any water,
we will count
how many your great presents
like numbering stars on the night sky.
One thing we do know,
you are always our Lord,
and shepherd who leading us,
and you are still the greatest.
We will see to tomorrow,
and a beautiful part of
your great plans for us.
Lord, we know we can trust you,
forever and ever.
Amen**

Faithfulness

My Lord, in so many ways,
you have led us,
you have helped us.
I heard their asking,
why would the people complain
comparing their life to others?
Why wouldn't they wait for patiently
your faithfulness?
My Lord, I am not relying on myself,
but trusting you in a wilderness of life.
I am staying in the prosperity of your
amazing promises in the name of Jesus.

"The Lord bestows on them a crown of beauty
instead of ashes, the oil of joy instead of
mourning"
(Isaiah 61:3)

I hardly know what to say about my future,
but I absolutely know how to reveal
your faithfulness.
I am looking what Jesus has done
through the word of God
and my life journey.
You have never abandoned me,
and you have never betrayed us.
Your heart for me has become my belief.

How might I be a servant?
How might I share your gift for me?
I love Jesus and trust your faithfulness.
I want to give to you my devotion
in all circumstances of life. Amen.

Garden of Memory

Lord of love,
are we in the garden of your memory?
Do we have that morning in the dawn
with the message of the resurrection?
Your remembrance through the Word is
loving, caring, and abundant
in comfort and mercy.
Before we met you,
we were always like an unnamed flower
blooming alone in the burial place of strangers
in the tomb of life.
But you gave us the scent.
You also gave us eyes to look beautiful,
and above all, people's hearts toward us.
In the morning of the Resurrection,
restore our memories as the joyful women
they met in your garden.
May your joy and gratitude be abundant
and full of hope
and love in the earth without peace.
We know everyone has a hard time.
Lord of love,
please meet us and comfort us at that time.
Jesus Christ of resurrection,
my Lord, my fragrance, my beauty,
I always love you. Amen

In the Field

Lord, in a world like the wilderness,
I put my weary self in front of
your shelter for a long trip.
Eternal Father,
in love with your only Son, Jesus Christ
please comfort my weary heart
and do not forsake me until this journey is over.
Lord of consolation,
always have a place in my heart
where you can dwell.
I am low and unworthy of the Lord,
but only by His grace
I confess that the Lord can come to me.
The world is always trying to get away from me,
but I want to get close to you.
Though people ridicule me and laugh at me,
always be friends with me,
He comforts me and makes me a true haven.
There is nothing in the wilderness,
but rather a place
where I can have intimate fellowship
with the Lord,
like the Exodus Moses,
where I can experience the power
and presence of the Lord,
because there is nothing to

depend on anything around me,
where I can see more of the Lord alone,
let me be there soon,
and be a place where the Lord is.
As a refuge for my life,
do not forsake me,
in a world like the wilderness,
where there is nothing,
let me rely on the Lord. Amen.

The Prayer of March

Jesus, the fresh air and sunlight
in March resembled our hearts toward Him.
The Lord of suffering and resurrection,
it is spring when the earth
that it has fallen asleep wakes up from sleep.
Please prepare this month
for meditation and prayer for you.
Let us be in the field of the cross,
and let us live in your garden with
those who sought you
in the morning of resurrection.
Do not follow this generation
but be a true worshiper with spiritual
discernment.
Lord of love,
with your love I want my soul to be resurrected
like a spring that fits the warmth.
Let me melt my frozen heart,
so that it may be flesh with the Word,
and be the March in which
the seeds are planted,
looking at the rich fruit next time.
I lay down all the parts of my life before you,
and I seek your guidance.

Pour out the oil of the Holy Spirit

on the hungry spirit,
and revive it again.
I believe that even though
many people leave me,
only you are God who protects me forever.
Oh! The days when we were poor
will turn into a moment of gratitude
for confirming your presence
with memories in front of you.
In this March,
I believe I can stand such a person
who is full of your love.
Amen

Praise of the Victory

The Lord who showed us
the perfect love of God for us on the cross,
your noble sacrifice has earned us
the path of eternal life in which we,
the sinners, will live again.
The Lord, who overcome death,
has overcome the power of death
and has given us hope of resurrection.
Thank you, Lord, for freeing us
from all the bonds of Satan.
Like the warmth of March,
when all things revive, with your love,
you will have the joy of reviving my soul.
Oh! May the Lord's warm heart
and gentle thoughts,
your power to break the power of sin,
stay within us forever.
Let all the world and all things kneel
before your name and obey.
Your love of the cross has made us live.
Our soul has been resurrected like
a calf from a barn.
Jesus of love, eternal Father! Praise the Lord
who is worthy to receive power,
honor and glory,
the grace to have the hope of resurrection

and to see eternal heaven. Amen.
You are the rock

You the rock to be avoided,
the Lord who always leads me,
you know my fragile appearance like a pottery.
Do not let me live in the world,
Hold me with the mighty arm of the Lord,
so that I can triumph and live in this world.
Father of power, the world is truly evil.
People do not acknowledge God's existence.
They like to dwell in the darkness
and enter the multitude of Satan.
May those who live in distrust
and have only eternal punishment
have compassion and know
that the Lord is alive and still in control.
There are so many who walk the wrong path.
Oh, Lord, You are alive.
You control everything.
Please fix this land. The land is getting sick with
pollution, war and disaster.
All creatures are sighing.
They are deceived by the evil crowd.
Lord! Please heal this land
and heal it with the love of Jesus Christ.
May everyone know that only faith
and love can live. Amen.

Prayer in the Spring

Thank you for heavenly Father,
for giving us the spring of warm season
and for your beautiful heart
that created the world.
I see your beautiful spring flowers
you have made
and realize your heart that is delicate,
everything is planned and accomplished.
Please melt my cold heart
and help me fill your love in me.
Help me to know the love, care,
and forgiveness of my Savior Jesus Christ
and to live in practice of His love in this world.
Have mercy on the many souls
who are still suffering
and groaning in the dark shadows of life,
and pray for them and become
the evangelist of the warm heart.
I pray in the name of Jesus. Amen.

Be Humble

O God, have mercy on me
and make me humble.
Let me always stand before the Lord
and have a watchman on my lips,
so that I may have the words, actions,
and thoughts that the Lord wants.
Let me remove all boast on my lips,
and live a life of exaltation and praise for you.
I want to put down the pride, lust,
and desire of this world.
Only you can be king and my master in my life.
I want to be a servant to obey the Lord.
I just want to raise the name of the Lord.
Thank You Lord, Sovereign.
I thank you for your love that you have always
given to me great things.
Just as flowers bloom and brighten the world,
so that I may be a disciple of the goodness of the
Lord in the world.
I pray in Jesus name. Amen.

The Life of the Evangelist

Thank you Lord, who is the living God,
the Creator of heaven and earth,
and guides all our lives.
We want you to always keep
your merciful heart toward us
and live by practicing the word of the Lord.
Like the Apostle Paul,
who reach the ends of the earth
and lead people to witness
the gospel of the Lord.
Many souls who still do not know
the Gospel are dying
and falling to the darkness.
Lord, we desperately want you
to remember the advances of all faiths
who have lived and witnessed
the Word of the Lord,
and that we can preach the Word,
build up Jesus' disciples,
and build up the Church as your body.
Lead us to be evangelists for your kingdom
and glory, but only us as instruments of
the word of the Lord.
Let all the vain greed
and honor of the world be laid down
before the cross of the Lord. Allow us faith,

and love to lead us into the arms of the Lord
with a lost sheep.
We pray in the name of Jesus. Amen

Prayer for the Oppressed

A just and righteous God Father
lead us to walk the right path in all our lives.
Let us look upon those who are oppressed
by righteous judgment, with a clear conscience,
and by the love of the Lord.
They are still suffering to keep a good conscience.
Protect those who are devoting their noble lives
to all the world's conscience and peace.
May the oppressors who oppress them
stand before the Lord
and make the justice of the Lord
so that they may be judged under
the law of the Lord.
They use their privileges, wealth,
and status to oppress.
Lord, we hope to show
the justice of the God toward
those who ignore the weak
and do not respect human rights.
Lord, you have always been with the weak.
You took care of the weak, healed the sick
and you became the Savior of sinners.
Lord, we desperately want to live a life like you.
Let all the poor in the world look round,
and become messengers of the gospel to preach
the love of the Lord,

and be a comforter for the weak.
I pray in the name of Jesus who makes the rich poor and riches the poor. Amen

Prayer for Everyday Life

Thank you, Lord of love,
for giving me the word of the Lord every day
and spiritually living in grace.
I pray for that to save me
from the temptations of the world,
and all the foolishness of honor and name.
Many people are going on
a broad path of destruction.
It is going to the temptation of the material,
and it is going to the wrong way
because the eyes are dark to the vain pleasure
and honor of the world.
Oh! Lord, God who knows
all my thoughts and hearts,
I want to live as a servant of the Lord for
all Your great glory.
Only satisfy the Lord, and live for the gospel.
I want be a steward to lead the wandering souls
of the world to the Lord.
The people of Israel believed
that the Lord was responsible for their life,
just as they have cultivated manna
and quail in the wilderness every day
and worshiped God.
I believe that you will lead my life.
Teach me day by day with your words

**so that my children do not get
the wrong way of temptation.
I pray in the name of Jesus. Amen**

A Prayer for Prosperity

I want the prosperity of my soul.
Lead me to live a life
that lights the dark places of the world
 by looking at the humble and gentle Lord.
I do not want everything to be good,
but let me trust in the Lord
with faithfulness always in the face of difficulty.
When my spirit is prosperous,
believe that the Lord of Immanuel
is always with me,
and that I may enjoy the peace
that the Lord gives me.
I look at all the wandering people in the world.
Have mercy on their souls,
and let them know that in the Lord the
prosperity of the soul is a great blessing.
May I always stay in the Word,
thank you for what I have,
pray for small things and trust in Him.
Everyone in the world!
Ask for the prosperity of your soul.
Our Lord is the God of grace,
the everlasting shepherd. Amen.

Recovery from Mental Illness

O! Praise God Father,
praise your high name and grace.
Thank you for leading our mind
and guiding me to peace through constant care.
With the power of our Lord Jesus Christ,
who has made the stormy sea calm,
let us bring a peace to our souls.
Let all fear, anxiety, and depression disappear,
and a calm peace like the sea that meets the
morning sun in our soul.
I want to be comforted by the word of the Lord.
There are many poor souls in this world
suffering from mental illnesses.
Like a young man who is suffering
from the mental illness,
and like a woman who has devil spirits,
many are wandering
without being able to adapt to reality.
Lord of love and power, have mercy on them.
May all the chains
that suppress the mind be cut off
and free from the forces of the evil.
The peace that the Lord has given us will be
overflowing in us forever.
I will sail safely to this world of steep waves with
the Lord as your Savior forever. Amen.

Prayer for Child Raising

Holy and merciful Lord,
thank you for giving us a home
and sending our children.
Please guide our children across
the sea of temptation
to come safely to the harbor of Your hope.
Help us the Lord to be
the captain of our children
and to lead them in the tempest of life,
no matter what test and difficulty they may have.
Let our children yearn for the wisdom and the
Word of the Lord,
and live a life of happiness
and thanksgiving in Him.
Give to themselves the strength
and courage to overcome
when they meet their exams,
and live in the grace of Jesus Christ.
May they always trust in Him,
even if they meet something.
Give your wisdom as a parent to them,
pray in love and support them.
Let them resemble the good heart of Jesus Christ
who honored their parents.
we pray in the name of Jesus. Amen.

Palm Sunday Prayer

**Jesus who came to the Savior
of the whole world,
Jesus who came on the donkey
into the city of Jerusalem,
Let us learn and follow your humility. Jesus,
suffering on the cross for all mankind,
and our Savior,
saw Him entering the city, saying,
"Hosanna!" Let us also be in the form of crowds
singing praise.
we want to find the Lord
who has been a true shepherd
to those who lost their way.
Let us know what true happiness
and joy is by shaking the palm tree this Sunday.
May it be a week of realizing the true love
and meaning of the Lord coming to the Messiah
of all mankind in this world filled with news of
war and darkness.
You are the King of glory,
the King of humility,
the Lord of all.
Let us resemble the humility of the Lord,
and be low and servant.
I pray in the name of Jesus. Amen**

Crucified Week

Lord of love, who prayed toward us on the cross,
I pray to the Lord during this hardship week.
I pray that your prayers of forgiveness
toward us will not be in vain.
May the love of your forgiveness,
who forgave those who persecuted you,
come upon us also.
May I forgive those who can not be forgiven.
May the power of the great love of
the cross be among us forever.
May the power of God's forgiveness be delivered
to all parts of the world in this afflicted week.
May your prayers of forgiveness
and love heal me.
Have mercy on us, who were in our own pains
because we could not forgive others.
Lord of Great Love,
I believe in the power of your blood
shed on the hills of Golgotha.
Thank you for saving us
and knowing the love of God forever.
Let us go the way of the Lord.
Let us love one another with the love of the cross.
I pray in the name of the Lord Jesus. Amen

In the Resurrection Power

May the power and hope of the resurrection
of the Lord be in me forever.
I desperately want to live
in the hope of the Lord's life
and the resurrection
as well as the beautiful flowers
that breathe again through the land
that freezed in the spring of all life
on this day of resurrection,
Lord of resurrection.
Just as God raised you,
our Lord Jesus Christ, on the third day,
so that the heavy stones
that block the grave in me
will be cleansed by the power of the Lord,
and the soul freed.
There are many people around us
who do not know the hope of resurrection.
Lord, let them also live
in the hope of this resurrection.
Let thousands of people who are caught in the
power of death believe
that the Lord, who overcomes death, lives.

On Easter morning

Lord of resurrection,
who has risen from the grave
and has overcome the power of death,
heal this world.
Let us follow the Lord
and carry the Word of God.
May everywhere in the world bear witness
to the Lord of resurrection.
Lord Almighty, protect your loved ones.
Fill my lips with your word and love.
I always want to live
and witness the love of the Lord.
But I am always weak and vulnerable.
I want to live the fragrance of Christ.
I always want to trust in the Lord
and stand on faith.
Let our children resemble Him and live
by victory in the hope of resurrection.
Let the words that always
come out of my mouth be words
that resemble the love of the Lord,
and always keep and guide them
so that our children can overcome the world.
I pray in the name of the Lord Jesus. Amen

Waiting for the Lord to come again

Lord of love and grace,
I want to overcome death
and wait for you to come again
for all the holy people on earth,
and to fulfill your mission.
I want to live as a preacher of the Gospel
throughout my life and to live
as a disciple of the Lord
who preaches the kingdom of God.
The Lord lives and still cares for
and leads the Lord's children like a pupil.
May I live the life of a holy bride waiting for the
time of your Second Coming.
Let us overcome
the temptations of the Antichrist,
and stand firm in the word of the Lord,
to keep the truth alive.
I always remember Jesus,
who promised to be with us
till the end of the world,
so that I can overcome all difficulties
by looking at the glorious state of
His coming in the clouds
and blowing the trumpet.
I am so grateful that you gave me your life
and made me live again.

I give you all the glory.
My God, Lord of my salvation! Amen

Pray for Husbands and Wives

Lord of love, thank you for giving us
a precious home.
Let the love of the Lord come true
through the home.
May the husband love his wife,
and the wife also love for her husband,
and devote and depend on one another.
Do not let any evil forces destroy our family,
and let the Lord lead us to victory in the world.
Holy One Lord, pity the families of many homes
that are falling apart, the ties being cut off.
let the couple live together for the glory of the
Lord for ever,
and good influence to their children.
Let our homes be full of God's blessings,
stand right on the Word,
pray always and be one.
We pray in the name of our Lord Jesus. Amen

Let me be a good parent.

Heavenly Father!
I want to be a good parent.
Let our children obey their parents
and lead them
to grow up on the Word just as
our Lord Jesus is raised
in the home and obeyed
Heavenly Father's word till the end.
Let me not be tempted by evil ways.
Lord of love,
may I love our children with His love.
Give me the power to control my feelings.
I want to follow the May I have compassion
for the weak,
who is always tempted to be tempted,
and that I want to approach my children
with patience and love of the Lord.
May I have compassion for the weak,
who is always tempted to be tempted,
and that I want to approach my children with
patience and love.
Let us trust our children and have a hope.
I pray in the name of the Lord Jesus. Amen

Let me be the head of home.

Holy Father,
thank you for being the head of a family.
Imitate our Lord Jesus,
who is the Head of the Church,
to make this family a church of the Lord
and to be the head of the family
in the words of true happiness
and righteous truth.
We are weak human beings weak
against temptation.
Lord, do not let any temptation shake
in your testimony,
and let me lead our family well.
Let me be an example from our families.
And let me be a leader
who can give unshakable confidence
in any situation.
Let me be governed by meekness, love,
and patience,
and a house of prayer and worship in faith.
Let us follow Jesus
in good conscience and heart,
and let us be happy in this family.
I pray in the name of Jesus. Amen

Pray for the World

Our Heavenly Father, who is our Rock,
the Lord of eternal salvation,
who always remembers us
in the midst of the world,
trusting God to accompany us
and standing on a firm rock.
Even in so many temptations,
we do not want our minds to change.
Just like His disciples,
let us live for the Gospel
and for the glory of God.
Let the wandering souls lead to the Lord,
and make them more souls saved
in the name of Jesus.
Let the political leaders of this land,
the leaders of the church, stand,
think of the weak people,
and become righteous shepherds.
Let us only confess
that you are the Lord who guides us,
and let us lead the world right
under the Word of the Lord.
We pray in the name of our Lord Jesus. Amen.

Prayer for the Magistrates

Lord, let the rulers of this land fear God,
lead the people in service,
and practice the justice of God.
Know that they will protect the weaker ones,
do not ignore the poor, stand on the right truth.
May those who do injustice
and those who do evil be far away.
Give them wisdom to discern wicked and
cunning words.
Please let them know
that there are still many alienated
and poor souls in the world.
May the cry of the righteous,
Amos Prophets still ring in the earth.
Let the law of God stand right,
and let good works arise to help
all people through right politics.
Once again we want to imitate
and follow the justice of Jesus Christ.
I pray in the name of the Lord Jesus. Amen

Let me be a good teacher and a disciple.

**Thank you for your gracious Father in Heaven,
who made this world, you are the ruler,
and you have led
all the loving children of the Lord.
Jesus is our true teacher, shepherd.
May all the teachers of this land lead the
disciples rightly.
May we proclaim the truth
and lead us not to go the false path.
Just as Jesus led and led the twelve disciples,
just as the Apostle Paul
brought Timothy to teach.
Let the teaching of the right teacher be made,
and let the disciples always respect
and follow the teacher in the learning attitude.
Let us lead in love and patience
rather than in our own interests.
Let us follow our everlasting teacher,
the example of the life of
our Lord Jesus Christ, the shepherd.
Education in this land is not coming right now.
It is a shame that disciples
do not honor their teachers
and see their right relationship break.
Lord, may they fear the Lord and stand above
the right truth.**

Let the broken order of the master and his
disciples be restored,
and let the right education stand
and honor one another.
I pray in the name of the Lord Jesus. Amen

Heavenly Father of Power

Heavenly Father of the power
to create heaven and earth,
always hold Your children.
Thank you for healing the sick with the Word
and for bringing love to the repentant
and bearing with the same heart as the Father.
Keep our daily life as
you have led the people of Israel
into the pillar of cloud and pillar of fire
in the rough wilderness path.
Let all the enemies before us withdraw,
just as you have defeated the armies of Egypt,
dividing the sea of the Red Sea.
May you be healed by the love of our Lord Jesus
who healed and saved many sick
and frail people.
May you trust in the power of the Word of God,
the power of prayer,
and the power of love forever.
Lord of the power, thank you.
Thank you for saving us
from the road of destruction.
Thank you for living as a child of the Lord.
Praise the eternal father. Hallelujah!

Let us have a tolerance for others.

**Lord, keep our hearts.
Let me not hate people,
but hold me in the love of the Lord
and approach them with a generosity.
Let anyone love and forgive
and pray for them like the Lord Jesus.
There is no peace in the heart of sinners.
They are always dark and uneasy,
and their way is destruction.
Lord, forgive us our iniquities
and let our hearts be full of joy and peace.
Any sinner is transformed
before the cross of the Lord
and lives as a child of the Lord.
Please change us.
May the world full of hatred, strife,
and jealousy overcome with love of the Lord.
I pray in the name of the Lord Jesus. Amen**

PART 2

Lord, where are you?

May all the things in the world be cut off,
and when there seems to be no hope,
find the Lord.
Even in the sound of the wind in the morning,
the Lord speaks with a friendly voice.
I hear the word of love that preaches me
more than a small bird on a tree.

Let me find you in loneliness
even if you leave me in the world.
Even in the hot sunshine of the day,
He protects me.
I hear that you will not hurt
anywhere in your body.

May my heart be found in the Lord,
my heart is not deprived of vain things.
Let us pray to the Lord without shaking
in the cry of a quiet grasshopper of the night.
May I see the beautiful image of the Lord
that is brighter than the moonlight.

A True Friend

When they all leave me and I feel that I am alone,
Before I felt this was sorrow He came to me.

Like the Lord of love, who came to disciples of
the Sea of Galilee,
You came to me at the end of this long loneliness
and desolate.

Standing alone in a frozen field, like a tree in the
frost and snow,
There was still a desire for a warm spring in the
stem.

Loving the Lord, you have restored a warm
heart to me in you.
I praise the Lord who has become my friend in
the long journey of my life.

The Peace of John 14:27

Lord I have seen a new light now
in the long wandering tunnel.
I do not know how many roads I have to go.
But I believe in the Lord
who will lead my path in this way.
I want to hold on to the Lord
who promised to be with me at all times.
The peace that the Lord gives is different from
that of the world.
The LORD says to me,
"Do not fear and do not worry about your
path(John 14)"
I put my worries and anxieties before the Lord.
I look only at you.
Oh! My Lord, let me go the way I should go.
Hold on to me every time I am weary and hard,
and the peace of the Lord has been in me,
May your love be revealed to all who meet.
O, my true leader,
the everlasting shepherd,
the God of love!

The Lord always listens

Can you hear me?
Do you always listen to my prayers?

Even today, I meditate and pray in the morning
before my beloved Lord.
My family, my brothers,
and many others want to receive Him and be
saved.
I want to tell them that the Lord is alive
and always with them.
May my heart be not changed to the Lord
even after all these years.

Do you hear my supplication?
Do you know my wish?

Even today, I stand before the Lord
and tell Him the hope of my heart unchanged.
Though I can not hear anything in my ears,
I think that the peace
and joy of the heart is the answer
He has given me.

Lord, as the dew of the morning stays
unchanged in my house garden,
Lord of love, I believe that you come to

my heart today and hear my prayer.
Faith in Focus on God

God, the Lord of the world, heals this land.
May our soul be found in this world
that is covered in sin and greed,
eyes closed to the Lord, and spiritually cloudy.

I hope that after long wandering,
our attitude toward the Lord
will not change all the time.
Let us get away from the things
that make us deceive.
Focus on God and restore our faith.

I think of Jesus' life in this land.
May you always focus on God,
and be interested in the poor and the weak,
so that you may find Him
who preached the Word of God.

Let us discern the Lord and Father of this world,
the false masters of the world,
and renew our spirit every day,
so that we may follow only our Heavenly Father,
our Lord Jesus Christ.

Walk with the Lord

I am going to live with the Lord Day by day.
I confess that the meaning of true happiness
and a better life is only to the Lord.
I hope that my heart toward the Lord
will not become a formal religious life.

Jesus Christ is always with us,
enjoying fellowship with us,
May every day be filled with joy and gratitude.
Far from making us sad and dark,
Let me come closer to You.

May I feel the presence of the Lord,
not the formal prayer,
but a prayer to accompany with Him.
When there is a test and a blocked wall
on all the roads leading to me,
Lord, give me wisdom, the touch of love
May praise and glory be turned to the Lord.

Praise the LORD, O my soul,
all my inmost being, praise his holy name.
the grace of the Lord forgiveness
and the power of the Blood.

The Heart of the Father who is perfect

The world without you can not give me anything.
I always feel thirst and hunger,
I can not satisfy anything.
Today I go on this journey of faith to find you.
I go this way to know my Father's heart.

You are the perfect Father.
I always learn the heart of my Father
who is waiting for me
even when I come back from a distance.
You have compassion, grace, patience,
and kindness.
I want to be like your character
and achieve perfection.

Every day before the Lord,
because of His gentle nature
Give me your peace over my heart and soul.
The things of the world do not give me
real satisfaction.
Lord, fill me with your character in me.
Let me live only with the Lord alone.

My Heavenly Father!

This Way

When my day feels like walking
on a road without light
Do not forget His steps that always lead me.
Today I lived a day with His grace.

Always be merciful to me, Lord, our Father,
Let me stand before your deep love to be a leader.
Even though all this walking in the dark
is rough like my night
My shepherd, Jesus Christ,
is willing to depend only on Him.

My heart is always in the light.
I am always looking at you like a bright sun.
All the paths I have to walk are
as beautiful as the cherry blossoms
that bloom in the spring.

I will always praise and sing in front of
you like little birds in deep mountains.
The Lord, who is always filling me with
insufficiency, will guide me,
Please be with me and always accompany me.

The Breath of Life

Let us live by the power of the Holy Spirit.
My life without the Lord feels like walking
in the wilderness every day.
I was lost in the vast earth.
I need your breath of life.

Jesus, my good shepherd,
came to your disciples after you resurrected
and gave them true peace.
And to them, the Lord breathed and said,
'Receive the Holy Spirit.'

Oh, Lord, let the Holy Spirit come upon me
and fill the heart and soul.
This world has no peace.
There is no true rest.
But I confess that
there is a breath of life
that the Lord gives me.

May this spiritually
impoverished world be revived
by the breath of life.
Heal the iniquities, rebuild the weak,
and let those in despair come to life
again in the breath of your life.

Living Water

When your heart is dry like a dry rainy season
and you can not find any life in it,
you should not despair that all the days you lived
were over.

The days will soon come when things
that weigh of life heavily will disappear.
We do not always have a flat road.

Faith is to constantly fight against
my rivals in me,
and when the drought of life comes,
I must go and seek out the water of life.

Let's look at Jesus. If anyone is thirsty,
we must go to the Lord,
and we must not forget the love of the Lord
who gives us living water.

Life is not so disappointing.
You who are troubled at that crossroads of life!

I will sing of the joy of salvation
in the river of the waters of water,
looking upon the eternal Lord when the grace
and love of the Lord come

before the Lord of Calvary.
Little Confession

The Lord who wants an honest spirit within me.
Your chosen person is in a cloudy world.
Through that many times and seasons,
there is a small flower
as if to make a flower on the spot,
although I am here in darkness and despair,
even though the rough mist is blocking it,
because of your holy spirit in me,
may I have a flower that is more beautiful
and vital than Solomon's glory.

When Life is Desperate,

**Think of him in the darkest
and most desperate moments of life.
Joseph of the Old Testament went to the
threshold of bullying,
loneliness, and death among his brothers.
Eventually he was sold into slavery to Egypt.
There was no peaceful life there.
He was imprisoned,
and in indifference he spent a day of pain in it.
But for him there was an attitude to life.
It is true to God. It is faith toward God.
We are weak characters.
It is those frail people
who can always easily betray the Lord
in a desperate situation. Do not forget.
Like Joseph, we have to trust in the Lord
in all circumstances and stand firm as a believer.**

**My soul is never disappointed.
I want to be a man of faith like Joseph.
Lord, I believe you are always near me.
May I not miss the line of life for Him.
Hold me, deliver me from this rough sea,
and lead me to the harbor of your desire.**

A Suffering Conscience

In the depths of my soul I try to hear
the voice of my conscience.
It has made me grow every moment of my life.

At the intersection of life
and every moment of choice
Sometimes I was suffering
from my conscience.

I always met the loving Lord
who loves and forgives me.
He took my heavy burden
when I was despairing
because of the sorrow
of my conscience.

My soul is now resting in the Lord.
Lord, my consoler, always gives thanks,
praise, and glory to Him.
Lord, do not forget me.
Please comfort me with sorrow
and restore the true joy of my soul.

Look at the Lord at the time of the test.

**Lord, who inspires my thoughts and wills,
May my heart for Him
be unchanged at any moment.
I hope you can always hold on
to your faithful heart toward me.
Give us wisdom to discern all the evil things
that make us not trust in Him.
If we are closer to the Lord, let us trust
and rely on your warmth that accepts us.
Let the righteous judgment and discernment be
in the Holy Spirit of God,
so that the heart toward the Lord
will not change even in the world,
and hold on to your hand and accompany you.
Even though there is no income, no fruit,
like the prophet of Habakkuk,
we want to be content with only one God
and live happily.
Our children also want to follow such a Lord.
My Lord!**

New Mission (Luke 24)

After His resurrection,
he came to His disciples on the beach of Galilee.
He was the Lord who comforted the disciples
who were desperate for the fear of the future.

The disciples recovered great joy
after meeting the Lord.
The Lord restored the mission of His disciples.
Lord, come into my heart and restore my
mission toward me.

Please give me a future as to what I should do.
Let us go back to the city with joy,
like the disciples who have met the risen Lord,
and go the way of the missionary
who is preparing the way of the Lord.

Lord, you are my God and my Father.
Do not let this despair be
at the end of your desire for the Lord.
Witness the gospel to all nations,
and live the life of witnesses who testify of the
living God.

Almighty God

The LORD God is greater than our wisdom.
Lord let all false dreams disappear,
and dream dreams of wonderful grace and vision.
The Lord, who is greater than knowledge
and greater than our experience,
is the Lord God.
Life, do not depend on yourselves.
Do not judge God with your short knowledge.
The Lord is always with us.
In any darkened circumstances,
the Lord does not forsake us.
He does not always forsake us,
as the Lord is with the disciples
in the ship where they meet the storm,
and calms the waves of every horrible life.
Your souls should not leave the LORD God.
God, the Creator of all the universes,
protect me and keep my children. Hallelujah!

The Lord is my Shelter.

**Lord, do not forsake me when
I am lost in the path of my life in pain.
When I am looking for the Lord
in the land like this desert,
take my hand and lead me.
Hear my prayer, Lord,
and let the abandoned people be comforted
by your grace and leading.
May you always be comforted by your Lord
and be glad for Him. I praise you,
my Lord, my shepherd forever.**

In a Dead End

I met a lonely, dead-end road.
When I did not know what to do there,
you came and said. Follow me. I will lead you.
Many people have passed by me,
but the Lord has always been with me.
I am not a small stone carved on the road.
I knew that the Lord's most precious treasure
and gift were me. I knew that it was my strength
to rejoice in the Lord.
This rough road has been a way of joy.
Everyone I met became a witness
to show His love.
Fly like a seed of dandelion
and let me live with joy
in any land the Lord will send.
I knew the path that the Lord had with me
was a road not to be lonely.

Depend on

Look at my enemies.
Look at those adversaries who are searching for
those who swallow like a crying lion.
O LORD, who delivered Daniel
from the lion's den,
protect me from the enemies.
Protect my children
from the evil influence of the world.
Give us spiritual discernment.
Let us defeat our enemies with wisdom and faith,
but only with Him. Lord of Power,
under the wings of an eagle My God
who keeps us forever, I will praise forever.
Let the name of God who gives victory be raised,
and let him walk on this path, calling on his
name.

Lord God, every day

Today I would like to live by your word
with the grace of the Lord.
I want my soul to revive every day
through your word and love.
I want my life to be restored.
God of the Holy Spirit, give me the wisdom
to live a day and make me happy even
in the smallest things. Let me share your love.
I am not lonely
because you always keep me by my side.
Fill me with your daily bread every day,
so that I may live and live in the world daily
while counting on you. Hallelujah!

Leave my burden to the Lord.

Lord of love,
you bear all my sin on the cross of Calvary.
I believe that love makes me stronger.
Lord, who came to this land
to bear the burden of sin,
I did not know the love
and I still wanted to burden it myself.
I have to leave everything to the Lord,
but I find myself not.
All I need to do is live in the light of His mercy
and love,
and I am still in the shadow of guilt feelings.
Lord, I want to put my heavy heart
in front of you now.
I want you to change my hatred
and guilt feelings
by your love and grace and joy.
I want to put all my burden down and follow
Lord. Amen

A Child of Hope

I hope that my fragmented minds
in the depths of despair to be restored.
The Lord is my rock.
It is a refuge for me in a stormy place.
Let my children hold on to the Lord
and not give up.
O! my Lord,
every time I look at the clouds of the sky
I know that you love me.
If I look at the wide sea,
I will see the Lord.
Lord, protect my children.
Let me have a hope for the Lord
in the desperation,
and never doubt that
He is always holding on to me.

Sail

When I am full of anxiety about the future,
I will remember the word of the Lord.
Do not worry about your tomorrow.
The worry of that day is enough for that day,
believe in God, and believe in Him.
Whenever my heart shakes like an angry wave
I want to know that the deep sea is always calm.
The more confused the world is,
the more I want to go deep into
the sea of His grace.
Lord of my life, Lord, keep me in this wave.
You will always be the protector of all the roads
I go and the road ahead of my children.
My anxiety and worry are not mine from now on.
The Lord is with us,
and I believe that this voyage will never be scary.

Satisfaction towards the Lord

I will look back at myself
who thought only of the conditions
for following Him.
Please forgive me for asking for more than
what I need, kindness and love,
and testimony of my Lord's love.
Please forgive me for waiting for more talents,
time and materials.
Lord, I have already given everything I need.
Let me live a day when I realize that
the Lord has already given me many things.
Help me to know that only one Lord is enough.

Cleansed Lips

God the Creator,
let me have a word of gentleness, faith,
and love in my mouth.
With patience, please give me clean hearts
and lips that do not sin before God like Job.
Lord, I am a weak man before you.
It easily falls into the temptation of sin.
I am going to the foolish way of grumbling
and despairing to the Lord.
God, have mercy on me.
Let my lips not commit sin with my heart,
and live in thanksgiving with holy words,
patience, and faith. Amen

The wickedness of the world is a moment.

May all evil forces of the world
be always part of the play.
May some day be convinced that
this evil reality is over
and the Lord's victory will come again.
Lord of Justice,
forgive me for thinking of the short scene of
the play and judging all of my life.
The Lord gave me noble life
on the cross for me.
He has given eternal life.
Thank you for your amazing grace.
When I am disappointed by the evil reality
in front of my eyes,
let me be restored to look upon Him
and always give me new strength
and power to overcome all situations.

PART 3

A Believing Family

It is so beautiful that a family is sitting around
each day and sharing the word of the Lord
and sharing the day's food.
The faithful children will always
be protected by the Lord,
and the owner of that family is
our Lord Jesus Christ.
When you awake in prayer
and become one with love,
the schemes of any evil will not bring down
that family.
Lord of the house,
I trust in the Lord and each other
in my family forever,
always keeps my family.
Let the righteous walk along the Lord,
and not judge the curse,
and be one in His love.
Let us speak each other beautifully
and comfort them.
Allow me to be honest and pure soul,
and rebuilt the ruined families of this land.
Hallelujah!

God's Will

You will find that the environment
and appearance are not important to the Lord.
Over the years
I knew they were important to the Lord.
But I find that all these things
are not important to the Lord.
What really matters is not what I have.
The Lord is more concerned with
how I work before Him than my work.
I realize that it is important not
whom I work with
but how I treat my co-workers in faith.
The Lord wants me to be worthy of the job
before the condition.
You are interested in me.
It is God's will for me.

Rely on the Lord

I hope to be a blessed life dwelling
in the Word of God.
I do not want to go
where the evildoers dwell on.
I hope that I stand firmly on the Lord's Word.
May the Son of God, Jesus Christ,
live in my heart and life.
The wicked deceive deceit and falsehood.
Let the heart be centered all the way to the Lord,
and allow faith like a mountain,
like a sturdy tower that does not shake like a
rock.

Morning Meditation

It happens to meditate on the word
of the Lord during the dawn of time.
It is a good time to focus on the Lord.
Let the first hour of the day be
before the Lord and be a worshiper.
I want to hear and to be led by the Lord.
I realize that living in the tent of the Lord
is the blessed life.
Thank you, Lord of love, always with me
and giving me this morning.
Give me peace of mind to my family
and let your peace be with me.
Let all the anxiety disappear like dawn mist.

A Warm Word

Lord, May I be a person
who can comfort people with a warm word.
Let me be a person who can give a positive word
and courage to a hearer,
rather than a rejection and a cynical voice.
Let us be disciples of the Lord
who encourage us with courageous writings
and hearts, like the apostles of Paul
who have gone on many evangelical journeys
and built churches and witnessed the gospel.
Please I want to always meditate on Jesus Christ
and follow his life.
Help me to give mercy and love to others.

He keeps faith children.

Lord of love,
let all their uneasy minds go away
and let God's peace be
in the hearts of our children.
Jesus loves children,
here is your precious child.
Remember always the children
who love the Lord.
Let all worries and anxieties disappear,
and fill in the innocence
and joy of childhood in it.
Let all the harassment of thought disappear,
and the true peace of the Lord shall come
in the sea as the stormy sea is silenced.
May our children grow well in His love.
Stand firmly on faith.
May all children overcome temptation
and triumph in trials.

The Lord who does not discriminate

**The Lord transcended race,
country, and environment.
We were created in the image of God.
I want to see Him in their image.
May all who love Jesus without discrimination;
treat all the weak of the earth without
discrimination.
Let us discard discrimination
against our skin color and race,
treat us with love, and build us all with the Word.
Let the earth be the land of peace
that the Lord truly desires,
and let it be full of peace and grace.
God who is just, God loves all people, wants us
to give up sin and follow Him.
Lead me not to commit
the sin of discrimination against people.
Jesus Christ of mercy, my savior God!**

A True Friend

All the friends of the world will leave me,
but only my true friend,
Jesus Christ,
is always by my side.
Our friends in the world meet
and break according to our needs,
but our Lord Jesus transcends all things
and loves me.
The Lord is a true friend of mine life,
and my Lord Jesus Christ,
who comforts me,
is the one who gave even precious life for me.
Thank you always.
I will give my life for the Lord.
Jesus as Friend,
My God as Comforter,
I will praise your name forever.

Keep your heart.

The source of life comes from our hearts.
Lord!
I want to keep my thoughts.
I want to keep my lips from false hearts
and unbelief.
Lead me to say the word of faith.
Let my thoughts always
please the heart of the Lord.
Even though life is the most difficult
and hardest situation
I do not want to sin with my mouth.
May I not follow the foolish thoughts
and actions of others.
Just meditate on the Lord
and give me heart and mind
to resemble like Him.

The Lord came to this world

**The Lord came to this world
in search of the lost.
Lord, I was lost before you.
But you found me again.
And you filled me with your one and only love.
Lord, until the day my life is finished,
as you have found me,
let me find out someone
who needs your help.
Heal the weak,
May the earth be filled with
your fullness of love,
just as you comfort the sad
and become friends of the lonely.
I praise my eternal God.**

The Way of Life

Heavenly Father,
I pray for giving me an honest heart
and righteousness in my heart,
and a heart that loves true words
and neighbors.
Let me not see the foolish things with my eyes,
and give me the heart to have mercy on the poor.
May our Lord,
who is a firm rock forever
and everlasting, keep a delightful inheritance
and the boundary lines which He has given me.
May the way of life lead us to the Lord
who has eternal joy. Please pray always.
I want to meditate on Your Word.
Let me be satisfied with seeing your likeness.
The Lord is my rock, the fortress,
the Lord of salvation, the eternal stronghold.

Witness

Lord, I will be the Lord's letter
everywhere I go and I want to be a witness
to the blessed word.
Let me restore my sincere heart in my heart,
and give me an honest and eager enthusiasm.
Help me to bear witness to the Lord.
May everyone in the world
believes in Jesus Christ
through my words and actions.
The gospel is power.
It is the light that can defeat all darkness.
Let us live by the gospel of the life
of Jesus Christ.
I want to be a person of the Lord
who leads the way by proclaiming the Word
and as the life of salvation.

Equability

**When my heart is troubled
I sing a song of the hymn.
Glory to the Lord with a beautiful tune.
A little heaven is right here.
There is peace in my soul
and all fear and worry fade away.
Last winter, the cold
and the storm have retreated,
and like the buds of jumping up
through the hard ground,
my heart is like that.
He gives me his peace.
He shows his love to me
and my young children.
Lord, you will always keep me.
In the Lord, I am not anxious.
You will lead me
till I reach the port of peace and hope.**

I will let down the nets.

"But because you say so,
I will let down the nets."
Like Simon's confession,
I will rely on the Word
and lead me to let down
the net once again.
I want to be courageous and obedient again,
even if I do not see any fruits in life.
I want to let down the net of obedience.
Oh Lord, have mercy on this man.
Receive me who doesn't have a faith.
I want to obey to your words.
Once again, come to me and hear me speaking.
I want Peter's confession to be my confession
and let down the net of faith. Amen

You know the wishes of the heart.

The Lord knows in advance
the wishes of my heart.
You know what I think and I hope.
I wish that be fulfilled in the Lord.
But my desire not to be broken
and my self are like a big rock
and I can not come to God because of it.
I want to rejoice in one God.
I know I have to abandon my boat
to walk on the water.
I want to rejoice in Jehovah.
The Lord knows the wishes of my heart
and wants to fulfill.
Let everything to the Lord.
I want to live happily in the Lord.
I want to put all that I have into the Lord
and to be Lord in me forever and ever.

Praise be to the Lord for eternity

The God of Jehovah,
the Lord of Immanuel who prepares all things
and is with us, glorifies, thanks, and praises.
We praise the name of the Most High
and lift up the name of the Lord who is above all.
Lord, always join us.
Cure, triumph, and encourage the race of faith.
May the name of the Lord be exalted
and serve the Lord alone.
Lord of all, save me and be my King.
May the name of Lord be praised forever.
Hallelujah!

Way

Where have our thoughts reached?
Who is in our center?
I am now on a wide wilderness road.
Beyond the steep hill,
I can not see what a city of hope will be.
Who leads me on this road?
I can not see with my own eyes
but hold my hand and try to believe
that this rough road is going with me.
Two disciples to Emmaus met Jesus of resurrection
and restored their faith.
Lord of resurrection you are with me
and keep me until the end of this road.
I want you to lead my thoughts, words, and deeds.

New creature

May God, the Creator God
who created all things by His Word,
bring the power of His amazing creation into me.
May all the filthy sin be destroyed
and a new creation born.
May the habits of pursuing
the sins of the past disappear,
that we may live with the Holy Spirit.
I want evil words, evil habits
and evil actions to be corrected.
Oh! Lord, I can not do it with my strength.
The Lord of creation can come to me
and regenerate me.
The Lord raised a sick man with a word.
Let the word of that power come upon me also.
May I only look to Him
and rely on His Word and live
as a faithful worker of Him
in the history of new creation.

The Lord's Family

Thank you for letting them know
that they are the family of the Lord.
I want to keep the word of God and act.
Let me be a spiritual family.
May all Christians in the world be
a family in the Lord.
Pray for each other
and encourage them to become loving families.
The Lord is our spiritual leader.
It is the head of the family of faith.
Hold on to our faith until the end
and let you depend on the Lord.
Let us not let our family fall,
but let us stand firm.
Let me be a house built on the rock,
not a house built on sand.

PART 4

Intercession

I feel that someone is praying for me.
Lord, my heart is always comfortable with it.
You have sent him to me
and have you prayed together.
I need a friend of prayer.
I am weak and fall easily,
but I gain new strength because of
the friend of the faith that the Lord sent me.
Pray for someone.
Pray for the names of those who need prayer.
Like Abraham's prayer for his nephew,
let me bow down before God.
He is the Lord who hears
the petition of the humble.
Let me not despair of those who pray more
when I am in trouble.
May I be grateful for those who pray for me
when I am happy and peaceful.
Praise our Lord Jesus Christ, the intercessor.

and let me not forget the Lord,
who is the friend of the weak in this land.
May I not boast about all that I have.
I want to boast of only one Lord in me.
I do not want to envy those who have
what I do not have,
and I want to be the envy of the people
because of the Lord who is in me.
I praise God, my eternal Father.
Let some people be proud of our Lord's strength
and comfort in front of him,
and let me live and testify of the word of the
Lord.

I want to hear the voice of the Lord.

**I want to hear what the Lord says
in this turbulent world.
May my heart toward you only focus on you.
Let me hear what the Lord's will is toward me
in spiritual discernment.
The Holy Lord wants me to live a holy life.
I want to live witness to the word of the Lord.
I want to serve the Lord's Church faithfully.
I want to be a witness to all people of His love.
I want to know clearly what your will is to me.
Only in the confused world can my heart be
directed to the Lord.**

Do not look back

Hold the plow in your hand
and do not look back.
I see the field that is still in front of me.
Look at the ground
and the rocky gravel,
and I look back what I left behind,
Lord, help me.
The painful memories of the past
have caught my skirt.
Where should I go?
The Lord will hold my life.
Whenever I look back
and regret, comfort me
and see the land I must go to.
Please keep my heart.
Please let me not regret
and see the land of mission.
Let us see the Jordan to cross
and the land of Canaan to conquer.
Give me courage and tireless power
that will not fear many adversaries.

O my soul, give thanks to the Lord.

O my soul,
give thanks to the Lord.
I praise the Lord,
who has not forsaken me
but has provided me
with all that I need.
He is always with me
and keeps my family.
Only the humble can appreciate it.
Only those who are meek, righteous,
and rich in love can thank the Lord.
Let me praise you with my faithfulness.
Let me not sin before the Lord
in any circumstance;
He was with me at every moment
in the past days.
Thank you for your warm guidance.
All the enemies are leaving
before thanksgiving hearts.
All problems will be resolved.
Give your thanks to the Lord.

Thanksgiving

Give your thank when you prosper
and when all situations are difficult.
Thanks is the most mature attitude.
A thankful man who knows how to love.
Thank and love are the same things.
Our Lord Jesus, always thank God.
He gave thanks to God for us on the cross,
and loved us and gave us life.
Thanksgiving is the best sacrifice
we can bring to God. Thank God.
Let us offer our thanks to the grace
and love of the Lord with all my heart
and soul. Lord, I want to continue to say
thanks to you from my lips and heart.
So I want to live our lives with thanksgiving.

My Children

Lord Jesus Christ!
Remember my children.
Please keep all the days of my children
so that they may live happily
in the love of the Lord forever.
You are our everlasting shepherd.
I want my children to be free to stay
and blessed in the green grass,
and to give thanks and praise to the Lord.
As King David, rejoice in the Lord alone
and be children to serve.
Lord! Remember the names of our children.
Let them not live alone in the world,
stand on the word of the Lord,
trust in Him in all trials.
Please remember our children.

Memory

I want to remember the grace
and all that you have done.
He knows the secrets of my heart.
He knows my troubles and sorrows.
The God of Jacob is my eternal refuge.
I want to live in the solid state of the Lord.
Forgive me my trespasses,
and let me always see thy righteousness.
Let my soul silently desire only God.
Only salvation comes to God.
Wake up in the morning,
meditate on the words of the Lord,
and begin the day with prayer.
I depend on the Lord.
Listen to my vows and keep your promises.

A Wilderness Road

God, who called Moses in the wilderness,
still calling my name.
I'm about to leave Egypt now.
To hear the voice of the Lord and to answer.
May my obedience to your word
lead me to the wilderness.
Both fear and worries about the future
are committed to the Lord.
He will guide my way.
May all the roads of this wilderness end
after the pilgrimage of faith,
looking to the promised land.
Where is my Mount Sinai to hear
the voice of the Lord?
I'll be there.
Let us go through this faith with strength
and obedience like Moses.

A Path

O God, when I choose a path,
I always want to go the path of life,
the path narrower.
Let not the wide path to
destruction lead to the ease
and comfort of many
but the way of the Lord
who led the people in the wilderness,
May God be our eternal shepherd
so that it remains unchanging truth
in the depths of my heart.
Lord, whenever I have to make a choice,
always pray in the Word
by the guidance of the Holy Spirit,
and let me stand by faith
on the conviction before God.

To Please Jehovah

I confess that it is my strength
to please Jehovah.
All the darkness and storms of my heart
will be calm, and I am sailing far
and wide into silence.
Let my joy be with the Lord alone,
and with the power of joy,
I will overcome the depravity
and the ruin of life.
May I give you everything in the world
so that I will not change my love for you.
The Lord is all mine.
Let me know now that
I am truly satisfied with my life.
Let all the adversaries around me go away.
Only the Lord is my joy and my life purpose.

The Center of my Heart

May the Almighty, Lord God,
help me overcome temptation because of
the Lord who is the center of my faith
every time I take the test.
I want to look to Him who is the center of
my heart and all my will.
I want to place the center of faith on my Lord
rather than on my experience and judgment.
Let me give hope to the Lord whenever
I fall and despair, and I will set my standards for
all judgment to the Lord when I am
in trouble and always making various judgments.
May my faith never change.
Looking to the Lord, I want to rely on
the eternal rock, the shelter, the savior, the love,
the horn of salvation, and the fortress.

Birth of Jesus

Lord, I am praying that
we will be able to spend the waiting days
for the birth of Jesus Christ,
who will come to this world as the Savior of all.
Let the world be a feast for the love
and grace of the God that Jesus was born.
May the birth of Jesus,
full of the peace of mind and glory of God,
be full of our lives.
Let us share the love of Jesus with
the weak and our neighbors.
May everyday life be a joyful
and graceful
and hopeful life waiting for the Lord.
On a winter night covered with white snow,
listen to the clear bells of the church hall,
and share the joy of Christmas with
our family and neighbors.
Praise the Lord of Immanuel.

Birth of a New Covenant

Jesus is our new covenant.
Through the new covenant of His Blood
that saved us on the holy cross,
we became spiritual children of God.
To this end, Jesus Christ came to this land.
O Lord, I will meet the Lord,
who is merciful and full of love.
May the joy of Christmas be filled with my heart.
Let us go into the light of the Lord's life
that reveals his righteousness.
Where is my mind?
I look in the presence of the Lord
in tribulation.
Baby Jesus of love,
May I have those who wait for your birth
on this holy night on a quiet night.

United to make good

Lord, I believe that all things
unite to form well.
I want to throw away all forms of evil.
Let us work together so that all forms of
endeavor that have been preserved
so far can be gathered together to form
the good purpose of the Lord
and to move in a good direction.
Lord, who touches
and heals our wounded heart,
I believe that the time will come
and the time of peace and joy will come.
I believe that there is a time
when the tears change
and the joy becomes.
As the Lord has come to this land,
we will see the land of hope lastly.
I believe that the Lord of Immanuel
will always be with us everywhere
and turn despair into hope.
We praise our Lord for making good
in every work.

Our victory

Our victory is
on the cross of the Lord.
I think of our great comfort
and salvation through His suffering.
I always meditate on His blood
that shed on Calvary hills.
I do not forget the hope of resurrection.
I remember as a garden of hope in which
rose flowers bloom all the time.
From there will be the Lord
who will hold us with his arms.
Blessed faith always gives new strength
and wisdom through the Word.
As all things are renewed,
the news of the birth of the Lord
will be passed on
to all the kingdoms,
and we will meet the Lord on that day.

Birthday

Thank you, Lord, for your grace
and providence in this world.
Thank you for sending my parents
and getting me to live.
There is no coincidence in the world.
Everything is inevitable.
The Lord has decided.
You also set the boundaries of my life.
Lord, I do not forget this grace.
Let me not deny that
I should always be in the Lord, that
I may cherish this precious life which
the Lord has given me,
and live for the lost and weak of this land.
May I always remember my birthday
and remember that it is a blessed day.
I thank the Lord for the position of my life.

Towards the Lord

Heavenly Father,
Lord of the whole world,
I want my heart to always go to you.
When I take the test,
I can rely on the Lord
and overcome it with trust.
Let us be free from the things
that make us weak and give us strength to win.
May Joseph, who has been blessed by God
in the land of Egypt, have dreams
and visions of faith in all the time.
We want to be like him in this land.
I see a lot of goose flies looking for a warm spot.
Through thousands of miles traveling together,
let me travel with my life without loss of dreams.
Let us live in the cold winter even in the night
when the whole world is covered with snow.
My heart always wants to go to you.

The Lord comes again

As the wise virgins
who prepare the oil
for the day that the Lord
will come again to this land,
I will wait for Jesus
as the Bridegroom.
I always want to be awake.
I rely on the resurrected Lord.
I want to live by looking at the Lord
who has won without despair.
The Lord will surely come back
to this land.
I do not want to forget
the grace of crucifixion.
I pray. Lord, give me confidence
and faith in my heart.
May I be awake, prayerful,
and ready, not to be tempted.
I will wait the time
when the Lord will call my name
and give my response to you.

Prayer

Let me come to Him daily and ask Him.
I want to be awake and prayerful.
I want to thank all things
and be happy.
May I pray for Him in any situation.
I want to overcome my trials with prayer.
Even though I go through the desert,
I want to avoid the despair
in front of the problem.
I always want to give a day to Him in hope.
Let me know clearly who I am before you.
May I live with humility in your heart.
Let us learn the humility of Jesus
who has come to the low place in this world.

The Second Coming of the Lord

Let us be with the Lord
until the end of the world,
waiting for the Lord to come again,
and be prepared everything.
Let us wake up in the morning
and see the clouds in the clear sky,
so that we may prepare the day with
a heart to welcome Him.
Let me first have the kingdom of God
fulfilled in my heart,
and the joy of a little heaven,
and live a thankful and a happy life.
May my daily life be happy
because of the blessings of the Lord.
I only want to rejoice in Jehovah to be
the first goal of our life.
I desperately want to preach
and teach the Word of God
and be filled with the disciples
who resemble Him.

A Word like Dew

May your words live
in meditation every morning.
May the word of the Lord come to
my soul like a dew,
as the dew drops all night
on the grassy leaves.
Let me immerse myself in the earth
and revive my spirit.
I want to live forever
in the living water of the Lord.
May my family does not leave
the word of the Lord.
May my wife and children receive
the grace of the Lord fully,
obey him, and live safely
under His protection.
I want the word of the Lord to be reflected
in every corner of my life.
I trust in you.
I believe that the One who is my eternal God
will always be by my side.

God of the Covenant

Because you are the God of love,
you make a covenant with us.
A contract is an expression of God's love
to protect us in this world.
If we do not have a covenant with the Lord,
we are those who have nothing
to do with the Lord.
Thank you, Lord that we can call God Father
as Father through obedience covenant.
Jesus Christ is the best fruit
and completion of the covenant of God.
We confess that we are God's chosen people
and covenant people through Jesus Christ.
Just as the relationship between parents
and children is created,
let us live through our Lord Jesus Christ
in the presence of God,
our spiritual parents. Amen.

Hymn and Glory

Our Lord and Father,
who is transcending all the time and space,
will entrust our future
to the beginning and the ending.
We do not know what tomorrow will be,
but God knows our future
and we will believe and follow Him.
Heavenly Father, I want to put down
all complaints and grudges in the satisfaction
and joy of real life. I thank God,
who is worthy to receive praise
and honor for eternity. Hallelujah!

Light of the world

O Lord,
I see the fallen culture of this world.
Satan uses all means to shield
the light in our hearts.
But I know that
It can never penetrate the darkness.
What Satan can do is to cover the light.
It's like a curtain in a room.
We know. Beyond the window,
there is always bright sunshine.
May the wicked not put curtains
in my heart.
Let me not be tempted
by the foolish seduction.
I will refuse the corrupt culture
and distrust of the world to continue
when it tries to shade the light.
Let me see the Lord alone.
Help me find the Lord of Light.
The darkness never overcomes the light. Amen

ABOUT THE AUTHOR

Yongjea John Han majored in Law and English Literature, majoring in theology in the Netherlands and the United States and Honam Presbyterian Theological Seminary. He also worked as a poet and writer in Korea. He then moved to Canada to continue his work as a writer and missionary. He and his wife and two children, near Chilliwack, BC, are dedicated to a mission for the weak and writing activities.

www.ingramcontent.com/pod-product-compliance
Lightning Source LLC
LaVergne TN
LVHW041630070426
835507LV00008B/538